THE LONG RIFLE

BY Robert Lagemann AND Albert C. Manucy
WITH DRAWINGS BY Daniel D. Feaser

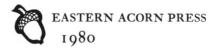

EASTERN ACORN PRESS
1980

LIBRARY OF CONGRESS CATALOGING IN PUBLICATION DATA

Lagemann, Robert.
The long rifle.

1. Kentucky rifle. I. Manucy, Albert C.,
joint author. II. Title.
TS536.6.K4L34   683.4'2   80-20797
ISBN 0-89062-087-3 (pbk.)

Cover: *Detail from* George Rogers Clark on His Way
to Kaskaskia *by Howard Pyle (1853-1911). The
Thomas Gilcrease Institute of America History and
Art, Tulsa, Oklahoma. Long Rifles, such as the one
George Rogers Clark (1752-1818) holds in this
painting, played important roles in the survival of
nineteenth-century explorers and pioneers. With fewer
than two hundred men armed with Long Rifles, Clark
captured British forts at Kaskaskia and Cahokia on the
Mississippi River and Vincennes on the Wabash River
(the site of the George Rogers Clark National Historic
Park). These victories helped secure the Northwest
Territory—Ohio, Illinois, Indiana, Wisconsin,
Michigan, and parts of Minnesota—when the land was
ceded to the United States in the Treaty of Paris
of 1781.*

Back cover: *Daniel Boone and two scouts exploring the
Kentucky River Valley. Mid-nineteenth-century
woodcut. New York Public Library Picture Collection.*

Copyright © 1980 Eastern National Park & Monument
Association

Designed by Winston Potter

Produced by the Publishing Center for Cultural
Resources, New York City

Eastern National Park & Monument Association
promotes and aids the historical, scientific, and
educational activities of the National Park Service.
As a nonprofit cooperating association authorized by
Congress, it makes interpretive material available to
park visitors by sale or free distribution. It also supports
research, interpretation, and conservation programs of
the Service. Eastern Acorn Press is the imprint of
Eastern National Park & Monument Association.

Manufactured in the United States of America

Contents

The Long Rifle 5

The Gunsmiths 7
The Pennsylvania Gunsmiths
The Mountain Gunsmiths

The Secret of the Long Rifle 14
Rifling
The Patch

Load and Fire 17
Ball and Patch
Powder Horn
The Charge
The Prime

Military Use 25

The Long Rifle at Historic Sites 29

Daniel Boone. *Engraving based on a painting by Warren Chappel (1820-1885). New York Public Library Picture Collection. Daniel Boone (1734-1820) and thirty men armed with Long Rifles blazed the famous Wilderness Road through the Appalachian Mountains and the Cumberland Gap in 1775. Boone's Long Rifle was decorated with his initials and the figures of Indian, deer, and sunrise cut into the butt. Fifteen hash marks along the stock indicated the number of bears brought down by the skillful hunter and his gun.*

The Long Rifle

In 1769 Daniel Boone crossed the Appalachian mountain barrier and penetrated deeply into the fertile lands which became Kentucky and Tennessee. Six years later he blazed trail for the famed Wilderness Road. Over this path would course the flood of pioneers who pushed the boundary of the United States westward to the Mississippi and beyond.

Like Daniel Boone, those traders and settlers who made the western crossing brought only what they could carry or pack on horses: a few tools, blankets, basic supplies —and the Long Rifle. The rifle was no less important than an axe or plow, and some would say more. It provided meat for the table; and, handled with skill and courage, it defended the tiny frontier settlements from hostile Indians. Long afterward, when the early clearings had become true farms, men still relied on the accuracy of the Long Rifle to control the wolves and other varmints that killed their livestock.

Today the gun is popularly known as the Pennsylvania, where most of them were made, or as the Kentucky, where it was first widely used. Two hundred years ago it was called simply the American or Long Rifle.

This muzzle-loading, flintlock firearm evolved from a short, large-bore rifle brought to Pennsylvania by German immigrants about 1710. Because it was a hunting rifle, it was often called a Jaeger (pronounced YEA-ger, German for "hunter"). The bore had spiral grooves to make the bullet spin and thus travel more accurately.

But hunting for sport in German forests was a world away from the realities of the great American wilderness, where the huntsman

5

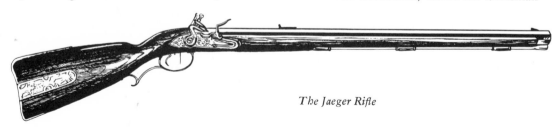

The Jaeger Rifle

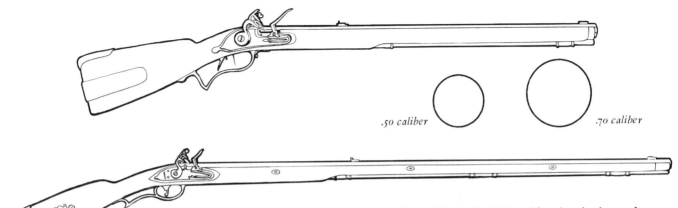

.50 caliber   .70 caliber

(Top) A typical .70 caliber Jaeger rifle compared
with a typical .50 caliber Long Rifle (bottom).

might suddenly find himself to be the hunted.
The American needed a weapon not for sport,
but to come by food and clothing and to
safeguard himself, his family, and his animals
from whatever creatures—human or otherwise
—threatened their lives. Had he listed the
qualities he wanted in such a weapon, he
might have said,

> "Make it durable and dependable (but not
> heavy or clumsy), accurate, hard-hitting,
> far-shooting, and sparing of powder and
> ball."

Out of practical American experience with the
big-bore Jaeger came ideas for improvement.
The woodsmen came back from the wilderness
to talk with the gunsmiths, and the gunsmiths
listened.

	The Jaeger	The Long Rifle
Length of barrel	28 inches	40 inches or more
Caliber	.60 to .70 caliber	.35 to .60 caliber
Stock	heavy	long and thin
Weight	about 7 pounds	7 to 10 pounds

The Gunsmiths

The Pennsylvania Gunsmiths. Soon after 1700, gunsmiths from southern Germany and Switzerland began emigrating to Pennsylvania. They settled mostly west and south of Philadelphia, and began turning out the same kinds of rifles they had made for their European customers. No other shops in America made rifles at that time.

These were small hand-work shops. In some instances the gunsmith made all the parts and fitted them together himself. Other shops might have three artisans who worked together: one made the lock, another the stock, and the third the barrel (hence the old saying, "lock, stock, and barrel," meaning complete). Every rifle was a truly handcrafted piece and therefore unique. Each smith had his own style, so distinctive that if you knew rifles, you could recognize his work even if unsigned. Many a gunsmith did "sign" by impressing his name or a symbol into the top flat of the barrel. It showed the craftsman's pride in his work and was good advertising.

For the rifle-maker, America was far different from Europe. In the Old Country, rifles were only for a few: wealthy sportsmen, professional hunters, and target shooters. But not in America. Here the frontier was moving west, and pioneering woodsmen fast became the best customers of the Pennsylvania gunsmiths. And as the pioneers pushed farther and farther from the eastern states and into the vast wilderness that would become the heartland of the United States, they came to depend more and more upon their rifles for survival.

For the pioneers, the Pennsylvania craftsmen made one change after another. Step by step they changed the stubby Jaeger into a firearm of truly American character—the Long Rifle.

The barrel was lengthened. The American rifles have long, slender, iron barrels, usually eight-sided. Most of these tubes are from 36 to 48 inches long, depending on the height and reach of the owner. Daniel Boone, for instance, wanted the muzzle to reach to his mouth as the rifle stood on the ground. (Measured by his last gun, Boone must have been five feet ten inches tall.)

The long barrel improved both accuracy and range. Increasing the length burned a little more of the gunpowder before the ball left the bore. With this added push, the ball went faster (almost 2,000 feet per second at the muzzle) and farther (effective up to 200 yards or more). The faster bullet meant a flatter trajectory (or flight). It's much easier to hit a distant target if you don't have to allow much for the drop of a relatively slow bullet. The long barrel also put more weight out front, so the weapon was muzzle-heavy and hung nicely while you aimed. And since the front and rear sights were farther apart, your aim was more precise.

The caliber was reduced. In comparison with the large-caliber (bore diameter up to .75 inch) muskets and fowling pieces of the 1700s, calibers of the Long Rifles were small, ranging from about .35 to about .60 inch. Most were about .50 caliber.

Because the frontiersman had to tote all his equipment as he tramped through the woods, he was practical about weights. For a .50-caliber rifle, every pound of lead he carried gave 36 balls—that is, 36 shots. On the other hand, for a .75-caliber musket, a pound of lead made just 12 balls. Furthermore, the small calibers took less powder per shot, so there were more shots from a pound of powder.

Gunpowder was precious. It wasn't wasted. *The stock was redesigned.* The stock, thinned down and reshaped from the Jaeger, helped give the Long Rifle excellent handling. A man could hold the long-barreled rifle at its balance over his left arm. The actual weight balance point, somewhere down the barrel from the lock, was often carried in the crook of his left elbow, with his left hand loosely grasping the lock area. This allowed his right arm to be free for other uses, such as to part brush in his path through the wilderness, to carry small game or an axe, to hold tree roots or rocks during a steep climb, or to hold the flap down on his bullet pouch when he was running so as not to spill out his rifle balls. Generally, the woodsman carried the rifle at an angle across the front of his body with the butt in front and the muzzle behind him. This was an easy, nonfatiguing way to carry a ten-pound rifle, and yet have it ready for shooting in an instant. He could quickly swing the rifle into aiming position with the curved butt plate hooked over his upper right arm near the shoulder, while sliding his left hand down the smooth forestock, and at the same time cocking the flint and setting the trigger with his right hand, all in one sweeping motion. Naturally, the rifleman kept his firearm loaded whenever it was carried.

The evolution of the rifle was well along by 1775, just in time for the pioneers to use as they headed over the mountains into "Kaintuck." The Long Rifle was easily the

Forging the barrel. Iron was heated until soft, wrapped around a rod, and beaten in the swage with an iron hammer to give the barrel its characteristic shape.

Swage

10

best weapon for the forest frontiersman, and it remained so for another five decades. With it, a man could keep himself well fed with squirrel, raccoon, or deer. He could kill an angry bear, a mountain lion, or stand off an enemy. Other firearms of the day—the fowling pieces (shotguns), muskets, carbines, pistols— were comparatively inaccurate, short of range, and clumsy to handle.

The Mountain Gunsmiths. Among the pioneers who moved to the western Carolinas and Virginia and into the Kentucky and Tennessee country were settlers who preferred to live in the mountains. Some of them were gunsmiths who brought along rifle-making know-how. Theirs was a skill handed down from father to son, along with tools, equipment, and family secrets in working with metals. Still, in the primitive isolation of the mountains, making a rifle from scratch would seem impossible.

But not so. Almost all the materials for firearms were already in the mountains. Iron, needed for gun barrels, locks, and triggers, was in the Cumberland Mountains. In fact, there was a foundry at the Cumberland Gap itself (the Gap was a natural passage through the mountain range near the point where

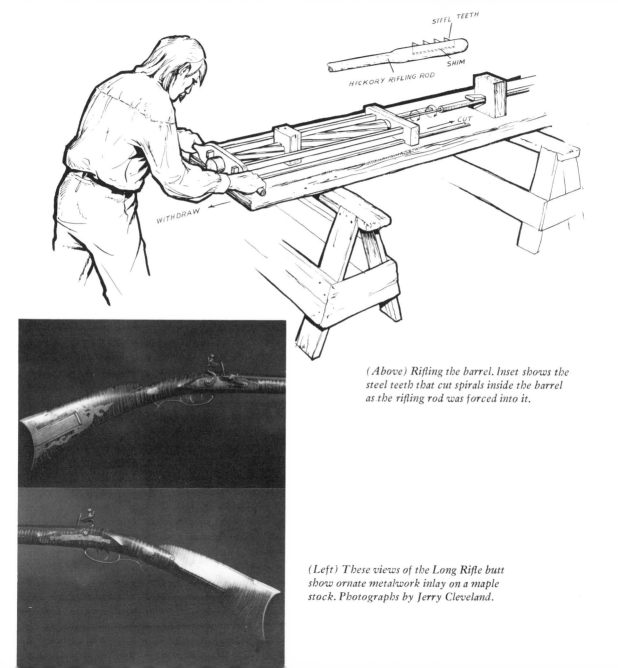

STEEL TEETH

HICKORY RIFLING ROD

SHIM

CUT

WITHDRAW

(Above) Rifling the barrel. Inset shows the steel teeth that cut spirals inside the barrel as the rifling rod was forced into it.

(Left) These views of the Long Rifle butt show ornate metalwork inlay on a maple stock. Photographs by Jerry Cleveland.

Virginia, Kentucky, and Tennessee meet). In the forests were walnut and maple trees for stocks, and hickory for ramrods. Local mines produced lead for bullets. Steel for springs came from worn-out saws and files. Only gunpowder had to be imported.

(Below) Fitting the stock to accommodate the barrel. The flintlock assembly is on the workbench in the foreground. (Opposite) Illustration from James Fenimore Cooper's The Pioneers *by F. O. C. Darley (1822-1888).*

So out of their own resources, the mountain gunsmiths made good rifles. No fancily ornamented pieces, but good rifles. The workmanlike simplicity of the guns reflected the plain lifestyle of the mountain people.

The technology of the times could not produce exact duplicates. True, bore calibers are usually between .40 and .60 inch, but there was no rule that said a bore had to be precisely .40 inch or anything else. On the other hand, there were practical standards. And nowhere are they labeled more realistically than in the Great Smokies, where

> a squirrel gun is about .35 caliber
> a turkey rifle is about .40 caliber
> a deer rifle is about .45 caliber
> and a bear gun is about .50 caliber.

As a woodsman's tool, the early Long Rifle was usually plain: no fancy brasswork and woods. By 1800, however, many of the gunsmiths were turning out works of art, graceful in form and ornamented in many ways: curly or tiger-striped maplewood stocks, elaborately tooled trigger guards and patchbox covers, silver sights, silver inlays, and skillful carvings. But underneath the fancywork, it was still the same fine weapon, prized for shooting accuracy.

F.O.C.Darley fecit.   F.Girsch Sculp.t

The Secret of the Long Rifle

We know a rifle is more accurate than a smoothbore firearm. But why is it?

Today the only common smoothbore is the shotgun, which spreads a cluster of small shot, used for hunting birds or rabbits. Almost all other shoulder arms are rifles. Two hundred years ago, however, most of the firearms were smoothbores. Except for small-shot hunting, these guns fired a single ball, which fitted loosely in the barrel. Loading a loose-fitting ball was fast and easy. But when the gun was fired, the ball bounced around and came out of the barrel with about the same accuracy as if you had thrown a stone. At close range you might score; but from a distance a hit would be pure luck.

Still, in the armies of the 1700s, soldiers were not noted for marksmanship. Lines of troops stood up and fired at each other, usually less than 100 yards away; and at that range some of the shots, whether aimed or not, were sure to hit. Generally the side with the most men and muskets won. The trick was to have them always on *your* side.

But the lone hunter in the woods could not count on chance hits to put meat in the pot. He needed a gun that would send the ball right where he aimed, every time, all the time.

Rifling. The spiral grooving inside a gun barrel is called rifling. As early as 1480 and well into the 1500s, however, a few European firearms were made with straight grooves in the bore to reduce fouling. Some researchers credit August Kotter of Nürnberg, Germany as the genius who twisted those straight grooves into a spiral which forced the ball to spin around its own axis, like a gyroscope. In the Long Rifle, the rifling makes about one complete twist within the length of the barrel. Generally there are seven or eight parallel grooves or rifles. The spaces between rifles are called lands. Spinning thus, it would fly true to the mark. Of course, air resistance and gravity slowed it down, but these were constants for which you could allow—except the wind on a gusty day could cause target scores to drop.

(Left) The spiral grooving or rifling inside the barrel made the lead ball spin as it was propelled forward. (Below) Lead balls, patch, and gunpowder ready for loading. Photograph by Jerry Cleveland.

In early rifles, the ball fitted the bore very tightly so that the lands actually cut into the ball. In fact, the fit was so tight that the target marksman sometimes hammered the ball down the barrel with a mallet and iron rod. For hunting, of course, this slow load was impractical. The pounding not only mutilated the ball, but spooked all game within hearing. The ball had to be smaller. Yet not so small that the advantage of rifling would be lost.

The Patch. By 1600 German hunters had learned they could use a ball smaller than the

bore if they wrapped the ball in thin leather or a tough fabric such as linen. When greased, this little package was easily pushed down the barrel. It fit very tightly (thus reducing gas leakage and getting the best possible boost from the powder charge). It gripped the grooves and thereby got a good spin and a stable flight. The ball came out of the rifle just as round as it went in. Moreover, the greased patch helped to clean the bore.

Once having found a good solution, riflemen stuck by it. The patched-ball load for the Long Rifle of the 1700s was the same as for the European rifle of the 1600s, despite great differences in the weapons themselves.

To load the Long Rifle properly takes about a minute. That's not really very fast, so you aimed carefully to make each shot count. In battle you might save 20 seconds by leaving off the patch; but if you did, you lost accuracy. In hunting, accuracy is everything. Patch the ball—that's the secret (along with eagle eye and steady aim).

15

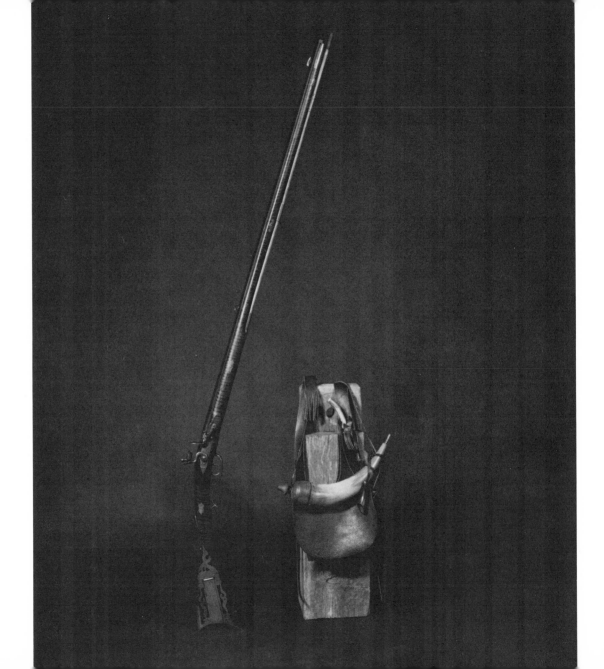

Load and Fire

Ball and Patch. The bullets for both rifle and musket were lead balls. The rifleman cast his own bullets, using an iron mold sized to his rifle bore by the gunsmith. Rifle balls were slightly under bore size to allow space for the patch. Patches, usually of linen, were cut into squares about twice the diameter of the ball. Some riflemen preferred to carry a narrow rolled-up strip of "patching" linen in the patch box (which was set into the rifle butt) and cut off squares as needed. Either way, the material was greased beforehand with beef or deer tallow, bear grease, or lacking these, spit. Thus lubricated, the tight-fitting patched ball could readily be pushed down the barrel with the hickory ramrod.

In addition to the rifle balls in a buckskin pouch slung over his shoulder, the rifleman carried spare flints, extra patch material, a short-handled screwdriver, sometimes a small horn of fine-grained priming powder, and always a short straight steel wire. He used the

(Opposite) Tiger-striped maple Long Rifle, buckskin pouch, and powder horn. Photograph by Jerry Cleveland.

(Above) Iron mold used for casting lead balls. Photograph by Jerry Cleveland.

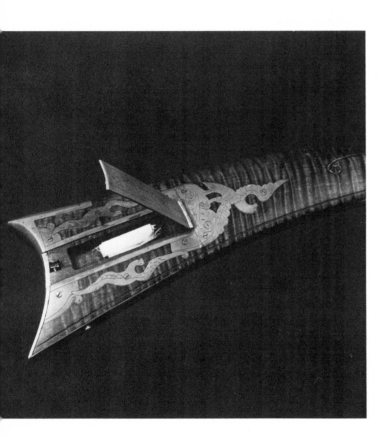

wire to pick powder fouling from the vent (touch hole) in the side of the barrel.

Powder Horn. A rifleman kept his gunpowder dry in a cowhorn. The horn was naturally hollow, did not sweat or swell, and it curved snugly around a man's body. To make it a powder horn, he soaked it in water to soften it, then plugged the big end with a carefully fitted wooden disk. As the horn dried, it clamped the plug tightly. Cutting off the point of the horn left a small opening—a natural spout, easily stoppered with a leather or wooden peg. The carrying thong, fastened to the horn at the base and neck, was long enough to sling across the shoulder. Or it could be tied to the bullet pouch.

Attached to the powder horn by a strap, and handily close to the spout, was the charger—a deerhorn or cowhorn tip. It was cut just long enough to hold the exact amount of powder required by this particular rifle for highest accuracy. For each shot, the rifleman carefully filled this measure level. Charging by guess would make his shots sometimes high, sometimes low.

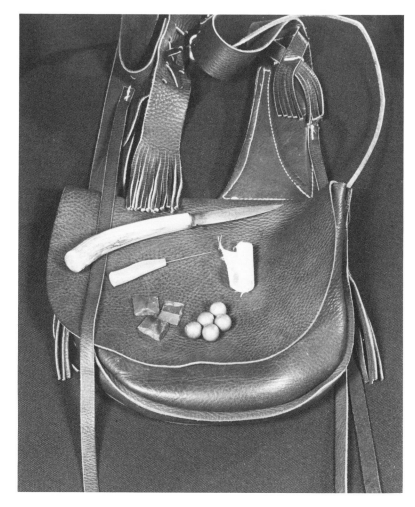

A typical buckskin pouch might contain (clockwise): a sharp knife for cutting linen patches, an extra linen roll, lead shot, flint, and a clean-out wire for the vent. Photograph by Jerry Cleveland.

(Left to right) Steps in loading the Long Rifle. Charging, placing the ball on the linen patch, seating the ball in the barrel, ramming, and priming with powder.

The Charge. To load a flintlock rifle, you follow a routine. First you drop the butt to the ground and crook your left elbow around the barrel to keep the gun vertical. The muzzle is near your chin, where you can see it clearly. Unstopper your powder horn. From it, fill the charger. Pour the charge of powder into the muzzle, then re-stopper the horn. Lift the gun momentarily, open the lid of the patch box (in the stock near the butt plate), and take out a patch. Drop the gun back to position. Stretch the patch over the muzzle with the fingers of your left hand and take a ball from the bullet pouch with your right.

Center the ball on the patch. Push ball and patch down with your thumb until the ball is flush with the muzzle. Carefully trim off the corners of the patch that stick out of the muzzle. (Some oldtimers used a big belt knife for trimming, but most riflemen kept a special small knife in the pouch or in a strap sheath. In either case, the edge had to be very sharp to keep from pulling or tearing the patch.)

Next, draw the ramrod from the thimbles and groove under the barrel, and push the ball and patch all the way down the bore until they seat firmly on the powder charge. Your rifle is now loaded, but not yet ready to fire. You still have to prime it.

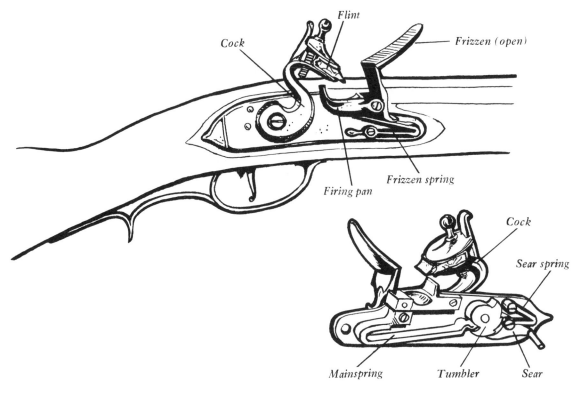

Flint

Cock

Frizzen (open)

Frizzen spring

Firing pan

Cock

Sear spring

Mainspring

Tumbler

Sear

The Prime. Pick up the rifle and balance it horizontally in your left hand so that the firing pan is at belly level. Pull the cock (hammer) back to half-cock (safety). The frizzen covers the pan. Lift it up. Use that rag in your pouch to wipe dry the face of the frizzen, the edge of the flint, and the pan. No rag? Try the tail of your hunting jacket. Then take the

Flintlock mechanism. Mainspring powers cock by pressure on tumbler (to which cock is bolted). Sear locks tumbler into position by pressure from sear spring. Pressure from frizzen spring keeps the frizzen either open or closed. Cock is pulled back in readiness for firing, tumbler revolves, letting tooth of sear into the middle notch of tumbler—the loading position. When cock is pulled back farther (into firing position), sear engages upper notch of tumbler and mainspring is fully compressed. When trigger is squeezed, sear disengages tumbler. Pressure of mainspring on tumbler causes cock to strike frizzen.

wire pick and clear the vent. Your dinner, or even your life, might depend on this step. With a clogged vent, all you get is a "flash in the pan"—no shot.

Now for the priming. Pour a little powder (up to half a teaspoonful) into the firing pan. Use fine-grain powder here, if you have it. Otherwise, the regular powder has to do. Close the frizzen over the pan. Pull the cock all the way back, and you're ready. As they used to say, don't go off half-cocked!

Of course, if you're at the wrong end of a charging bear, you could skip wiping the lock and maybe even cleaning the vent. But always, *always* prime the pan, close the frizzen, and pull the cock.

When you squeeze the trigger, here's what happens:
1. The cock springs forward.
2. Flint strikes the steel frizzen, making sparks.
3. As the frizzen bounds up from the blow, it exposes the powder in the pan to the sparks.
4. The powder in the pan flashes, sending a jet of flame through the vent into the barrel. The powder in the barrel ignites, and its sudden, expanding gas pushes the ball out of the barrel at high speed.

Don't pull that trigger until your sights are on target.

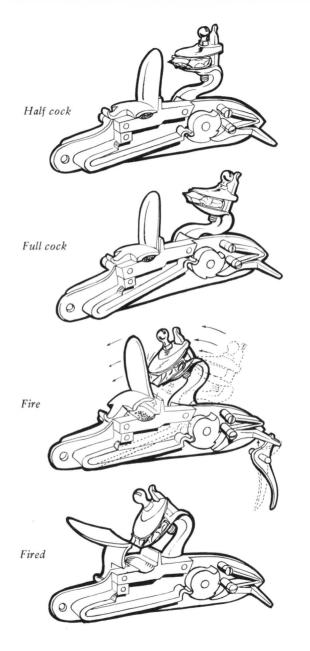

Half cock

Full cock

Fire

Fired

The Battle of Kings Mountain *(October 7, 1780)*. *Engraving after Chappel's painting. New York Public Library Picture Collection.*

Military Use

The Long Rifle made it possible for families to settle the grasslands and forests from the Appalachians to the Mississippi and from the Great Lakes to the Gulf of Mexico. It was the hunter's constant companion, the settler's dependable tool, and defender of the frontier.

Why, then, didn't the army use it?

Armies did use it, but not very much. There were some good reasons: (1) The rifle was slow to load. A soldier could fire a musket three times as fast. (2) The Long Rifle took longer to make, and cost more than a musket. (3) Rifle calibers varied so much that supplying ammunition for an army of riflemen would be a real problem. (4) Muskets withstood a soldier's rough handling better than rifles. (5) Rifles did not take bayonets. Muskets did, and the bayonet often decided the battle outcome. So for the most part, the military used rifles only for specialized work, such as sharpshooting at marks far beyond musket range or accuracy.

As a matter of fact, ten companies of "expert riflemen" were recruited for the

American Rifleman 1775

American Rifleman 1814

American army in 1775. George Rogers Clark's men carried Long Rifles in 1779 at the capture of the British Fort Sackville at Vincennes on the Wabash River. By aiming at the fort loopholes and embrasures, the American sharpshooters picked off the defenders one by one. Indeed, given the right circumstances, the rifle was a spectacular weapon. In the Carolina campaign, a British officer wrote that he "never in my life saw better rifles (or men who shot better) than those made in America." One sharpshooter, he said, drew a bead on a trio of mounted men 400 yards away. His shot hit dead center, killing the horse of the man in the middle.

The most convincing rifle victory of the American Revolution took place at Kings Mountain, South Carolina. Major Patrick Ferguson of the British Army headed a scouting force of 1,100 men, and made the mistake of boasting to the mountaineers that he would "march an army over the mountains, hang their leaders, and lay their country waste." Like a swarm of hornets Americans surrounded Ferguson's camp on October 7, 1780. The patriot force, 910 riflemen, pressed up the forested slopes, taking advantage of the natural cover. The fight lasted just an hour. The rifles killed Ferguson and 225 of his men

The Hunters of Kentucky as Sung in Character by Mr. PETRIE with unbounded applause at Chatham Garden Theatre the Symphonies & Accompaniments. WILLIAM BLONDELL.

This song, which popularized Andrew Jackson's success in the fight against the British, later became Jackson's campaign song when he ran for the presidency. Courtesy of Lester S. Levy.

and wounded 163; the rest were captured. Of the mountain men, only 28 were killed and 62 wounded.

A few decades later, in the hands of Andrew Jackson's Tennesseeans, the Long Rifle won other important battles. At Horseshoe Bend, Alabama, Jackson's marksmen scourged the Red Stick faction of the Creek Indians in 1814 and thus opened the Alabama country to pioneer settlement. On a frosty January day nine months later, Jackson and his regulars, plus a motley array of volunteer riflemen, Creoles, blacks, sailors, and ex-pirates waited behind a mud wall as an army of 5,000 crack British troops advanced across a stubbled canefield near New Orleans. The Americans opened fire with rifles and artillery, but the British came on . . . and on . . . until 2,000 of their 5,000 had fallen. Incredibly, American losses were only seven killed, six wounded.

The Battle of New Orleans *(January 8, 1815). Engraving after a painting by D. M. Carter (1827-1881).*
New York Public Library Picture Collection.

The Long Rifle at Historic Sites

The role of the Long Rifle on the western frontier was a major one. With it, Americans had settled the lands beyond the mountains as far as the Mississippi by the 1830s. But it was inevitable that improvements in gun design, ignition systems, and ammunition would make the Long Rifle obsolete.

In 1803 the Harpers Ferry Arsenal (its ruins now part of Harpers Ferry National Historical Park, West Virginia) began making the first regulation rifles for the United States Army. This M1803 was short-barreled (33 inches) and kicked like a mule, but in the military it supplanted the Long Rifle. Within the next 20 years the army carried this gun deep into the territory that became South Dakota, Kansas, Nebraska, Colorado, New Mexico, Oklahoma, Arkansas, and Texas.

Outside the military, however, the Long Rifle for many years remained the basic tool for those intrepid souls who made their living in the wilderness of the heartland—the trappers and the traders as well as those who chose to settle on the land. In fact, after 1820 the Old

Reliable was made even more reliable with a percussion cap lock instead of the ancient flint lock. Nevertheless, the heyday of the Long Rifle ended as technological advances made breech-loaders practical and eventually produced efficient repeating rifles.

The Long Rifle is part of the story at numerous areas in the National Park system. Cumberland Gap National Historical Park (Kentucky, Tennessee, and Virginia) is one of them. Following Daniel Boone's trail, thousands of settlers passed through the Cumberland Gap to make new homes beyond the Appalachians. For most of them, the rifles they carried meant survival. At Cumberland Gap, too, are the remains of a foundry that provided iron to make these rifles and other essential tools.

Great Smoky Mountains National Park (North Carolina and Tennessee) is not only one of the great natural scenic reserves, but features the culture and crafts of the mountain people, as do Shenandoah National Park (Virginia) and the Blue Ridge Parkway

(North Carolina and Virginia) connecting the two parks. Historical markers along the parkway bear a silhouette of the Long Rifle, reminding us of its importance to the mountain people. Not many who drive the parkway today realize that in 1780 over-the-mountain settlements on the Watauga and Holston rivers of Tennessee sent their rifle-toting citizens to stop the British in South Carolina. The routes these men took on their way to Kings Mountain cross the present Parkway in a number of places.

The action at Kings Mountain showed the deadly effectiveness of the Long Rifle in the hands of brave and resourceful frontiersmen who were determined to protect their homes and loved ones from British invasion. Kings Mountain National Military Park (South Carolina) preserves the site of the battle.

An earlier (1778-1779) achievement is seen at George Rogers Clark National Historical Park (Indiana). The park contains the site of British Fort Sackville and memorializes Clark's rifle-armed expedition and its effect on the winning of the Old Northwest (the present states of Ohio, Indiana, Illinois, Wisconsin, and Michigan).

Other sites where the American rifle was a deciding factor include Horseshoe Bend National Military Park (Alabama), where in 1814 Jackson's defeat of the Creeks opened the Old Southwest to settlement; and the Chalmette unit of Jean LaFitte National Historical Park (Louisiana), which was the scene of the Battle of New Orleans in 1815.

Natchez Trace Parkway (Alabama, Mississippi, and Tennessee) traverses the pioneer trail from Natchez to Nashville. Ohio Valley boatmen used the Ohio and Mississippi rivers to float their cargoes down to New Orleans. Because they couldn't float upriver against the current, they "traced" or followed a trail on land and returned home by foot. And via the Natchez Trace, too, came Andrew Jackson, marching his Tennessee riflemen back from the Battle of New Orleans.

Perhaps we should also mention Mammoth Cave National Park (Kentucky). It was from the cave that workmen took petredirt—an essential ingredient of gunpowder—for the powder mills of the 1812 war.

Fort Smith National Historic Site (Arkansas) features the opening of the West and preserves the remains of two successive frontier forts built in 1817 and 1828. When the Rocky Mountain fur trade was at its height during the early 1830s, Bent's Old Fort (Colorado) was an important center. Fort Laramie

National Parks where the Long Rifle played a part.

(Wyoming) was a fur trading post established in 1834. Later it became a military base guarding the wagon trails to Oregon and California. Fort Union (North Dakota) was a major hub of the fur trade for almost 50 years. Each of these posts is now a national historic site. The story of the pioneers who settled the West is the theme of Jefferson National Expansion Memorial at St. Louis, Missouri.

But who can list all the places and occasions the Long Rifle made history? For rather than a weapon of war, it was the frontiersman's survival tool: sighting down the barrel, he could kill a deer as far away as 150 yards. The same Long Rifle, if it is in good condition, can still hold its own at marks up to 100 yards.

In its day and realm, the Long Rifle was the most accurate firearm in the world.

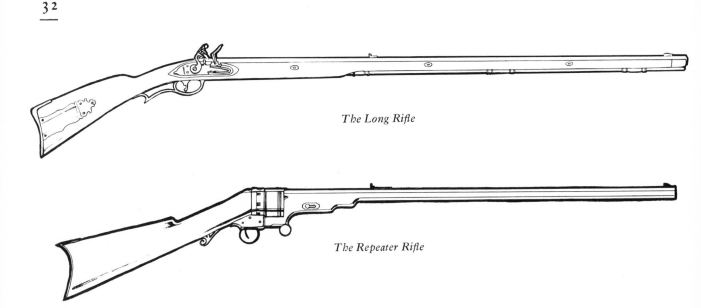

The Long Rifle

The Repeater Rifle